The

LITTLE BOOK OF
CONSPIRACY
THEORIES

THE LITTLE BOOK OF CONSPIRACY THEORIES

An Hachette UK Company
www.hachette.co.uk

Summersdale Publishers
Part of Octopus Publishing Group Limited
Carmelite House
50 Victoria Embankment
LONDON
EC4Y 0DZ
UK

www.summersdale.com

Printed and bound in Poland

ISBN: 978-1-83799-436-6

This FSC® label means
that materials used for
the product have been
responsibly sourced

MIX
Paper | Supporting
responsible forestry
FSC® C018236

Substantial discounts on bulk quantities of Summersdale books are available to corporations, professional associations and other organizations. For details contact general enquiries: telephone: +44 (0) 1243 771107 or email: enquiries@summersdale.com.

The

LITTLE BOOK OF

CONSPIRACY

THEORIES

Jamie King

summersdale

Contents

Introduction

Welcome to *The Little Book of Conspiracy Theories*. If you have ever wondered what secrets are lurking beyond the gates of Area 51, if you have ever questioned who was really behind the assassination of JFK or if you have never been convinced that the Moon landings did in fact take place, you are in good company. Collected in this little book are some of the wackiest, weirdest and most worrying conspiracy theories ever to have circulated.

At the heart of any good conspiracy theory is the belief that things are not what they seem – that some influential person or organization is responsible for orchestrating events and covering their tracks. And any good conspiracy theorist knows to look for explanations for the unexplained and never to trust what the government says.

Some of the theories gathered here – such as the belief in the existence of a race of people living inside the hollow centre of our planet and that Elvis is still alive – may seem harmless enough. Others have arguably contributed to real-world harm. We hope you have fun reading – but don't fall too far down the rabbit hole.

POLITICAL AND GOVERNMENTAL

Politicians don't have the best reputation for being truthful – and more than a few have been caught out in a lie over the years. It's therefore hardly surprising that there are such a great number of conspiracy theories concerning governments. Who knows what they could be planning? What shady groups are pulling the strings in the shadows of the corridors of power? Some of the theories in this chapter – such as those surrounding *The Protocols of the Elders of Zion* – stretch back for centuries. Others, like those circulated by the shadowy figure(s) known as "QAnon", are rooted in our modern times of social media and fake news. All the theories in this chapter have in common a deep-rooted mistrust of the ruling elite. That might not be such a bad thing, if those who believe our leaders are shapeshifting reptilians turn out to be right.

NEW WORLD ORDER

WHO:
A secretive power elite

WHEN:
Middle Ages to present day

WHAT:
The elite is conspiring to achieve global
domination and rule the world through
an authoritarian one-world government

How it began

The New World Order. Sounds like some sort of 1980s boy band, doesn't it? But it may be something far more sinister. According to conspiracy theorists, a powerful group of individuals has been manipulating the course of global events for centuries as part of their plot to take over the world and establish an authoritarian One World Government. This cabal is believed to be made up of politicians, the world's richest people and aristocracy. Some conspiracists trace it back to 13 genetically related families, referred to as the Illuminati. Working behind the scenes in the corridors of power, this shadowy group aims to create a feudalist state in which there is no middle class, only a ruling class and a servant class. In this One World Government there would be no national and regional borders. It would operate using a single monetary system and be policed by a One World Government unified military. In this new, despotic world, only the subservient would survive.

With them or against them?

Proponents of the theory believe that the leaders of most modern industrialized countries are members of or are in collusion with the cabal, whose influence also extends to major captains of industry in sectors such as oil, banking and pharmaceuticals. The reason so many have joined its ranks is simple: anyone who is against them must be eliminated. Examples of influential figures who have purportedly gone against the cabal's desires and constitute a threat to its power base include John F. Kennedy and his brother Robert, whose assassinations are said by conspiracists to have been orchestrated by the Illuminati. Ali Bhutto (the founder of the Pakistan People's Party) and, more recently, his daughter Benazir are also believed to have been targeted. Bhutto Sr. was executed, Bhutto Jr. was assassinated. The list of prominent figures whose ideals have allegedly clashed with those of the Illuminati is long and includes individuals who have fought for peace, such as John Lennon.

Population control

A main aim of those who seek to establish the New World Order, so conspiracists claim, is to reduce the human population as much as possible, perhaps even to as little as one billion people. A smaller population would be easier to control, apparently, and would also place less of a burden on the Earth's dwindling natural resources. Theorists therefore have been quick to blame the cabal for many historical events that have involved large losses of life, going back as far as the Crusades in the Middle Ages, and in modern times events such as the two World Wars, the Great Depression of the 1930s, the Korean War, the Vietnam War, the fall of the Soviet empire, both Gulf Wars, the Balkans War, the countless conflicts in Africa and the Middle East, the Boxing Day tsunami, the 2007–2009 global recession, the Covid-19 pandemic – you name it and, as theorists claim, these shadowy power figures have probably had a hand in it.

Mind control

The power games reach into all corners of our lives – even our minds. Conspiracists claim that the power elite seeking to establish the New World Order is responsible for manufacturing a culture of fear because a mistrustful and mutually fearing population is easier for those in power to control. And that's only the beginning. It is feared that the power elite will implement a broad range of tactics to subvert individuals' control of their own thoughts, behaviour, emotions and decisions. The methods they are said to have employed include:

- Brainwashing techniques such as those trialled in the US's controversial Project MKULTRA.
- Water fluoridation.
- Subliminal advertising.
- Electronic harassment via microwave signals, including the use of MEDUSA, a directed-energy non-lethal weapon.

THE NORTH AMERICAN UNION

WHO:

A mysterious global elite

WHEN:

Mid-1990s–present

WHAT:

A secret plan to combine the USA,
Canada and Mexico into a superstate

How it began

Since the early 1990s, when the Maastricht Treaty was signed and the North American Free Trade Agreement (NAFTA) came into being, there have been rumours about the creation of a North American Union (NAU), similar to the European Union, in which the governments in Washington, Ottawa and Mexico City would be replaced by a centralized political system. Following the formation of the Security and Prosperity Partnership of North America in 2005, these theories picked up pace. According to the conspiracists, the NAU would be accomplished by stealth in the form of a string of free trade agreements. Conservative commentators Phyllis Schlafly, Jerome Corsi and Howard Phillips set up a website dedicated to quashing the concept of a NAU in 2006. In 2008, discussion about the potential implementation of a NAU became so widespread that it came up as a topic of debate during the US presidential election campaigns and was the subject of various US Congress resolutions.

A united continent

Two prominent features of the new NAU, theorists believe, would be the creation of a single currency and a gigantic 12-lane superhighway linking Canada, the USA and Mexico. This "super corridor" would stretch all the way from the Yukon to the Yucatan and would allow for the easy movement of trade and people within the superstate's new, expanded borders. The new currency would be called the Amero, replacing the US and Canadian dollars and the Mexican peso. This idea actually dates back to *The Case for the Amero,* published by Canadian economist Herbert G. Grubel in 1999. In 2007, two conspiracy theorists, Hal Turner and Ace Sabau, claimed that they had convinced an employee of the US Treasury Department to smuggle out a United States government minted "amero" coin. Some theorists claim Spanish would replace English as the primary language used in most official settings, pointing to the growth of the Hispanic population in the US.

Who could be behind it?

Conspiracy theorists believe that the NAU concept has been created by liberal industrialists who would benefit from the trade freedoms that the union would precipitate. They argue that these industrialists are attempting to achieve their goal through a series of trade arrangements, and that the activities of the North American Free Trade Agreement (NAFTA) and the Council on Foreign Relations (CFR) are geared towards the realization of the NAU. The North American SuperCorridor Coalition (NASCO) has also been implicated by theorists. This organization's mission is to support business along a trade corridor that stretches from eastern and central Canada through the central US and into Mexico. Other conspiracists speculate that the NAU is a red herring created by right-wing business groups in the US to divert attention away from real issues facing the country, such as racial tension, illegal immigration and unemployment.

The official line

While rumours of the impending NAU abounded in the mid-2000s, officials were quick to deny that they held any weight:

- In 2007, US Commerce Secretary Carlos Gutierrez stated: "There is no secret plan to create a North American union, or a common currency, or to intrude on the sovereignty of any of the partner nations".

- The Federal Highway Administration have denied the existence of a NAFTA superhighway scheme, while NASCO denies that there are proposals for such a road, saying that it already exists as I-35.

- In August 2007, Canadian Prime Minister Stephen Harper said that he didn't think that the NAU was a "generally expressed concern", while US President George W. Bush decried discussions of a NAU as "comical" and "political scare tactics".

WHO:

Online conspiracy theorists
posting on the website 4chan

WHEN:

2017–present

WHAT:

Then President Donald Trump was
waging a secret war against a cabal of
paedophiles and the so-called "deep state"

How it began

QAnon emerged from the Pizzagate conspiracy theory. During the 2016 election campaign, the online whistleblower WikiLeaks released emails that Russian hackers had stolen from the account of John Podesta, Hillary Clinton's campaign chair. In several of these emails "cheese pizza" was mentioned, which theorists posting on the forum website 4chan believed was code for "child pornography". This evolved into the idea that a pizzeria Podesta had ordered from, Comet Ping Pong, was the centre of a child sex trafficking ring run by an elite cabal of satanic cannibals. On 28 October 2017, a post by an unidentified individual, or group of individuals, calling themselves Q appeared on 4chan, falsely claiming that Hillary Clinton was about to be arrested. Q later claimed to be a government official with links to the Trump administration and that Trump would launch an attack on deep-state officials responsible for the paedophile ring involved in Pizzagate. The conspiracy theory arising from these claims became known as QAnon.

Trump's involvement

The QAnon conspiracy theorists expanded their theories over time to reflect world events. Trump supporters and even Trump himself sometimes echoed QAnon beliefs, as was the case with the infamous Covid-19 bleach remedy. QAnon theorists suggested that drinking industrial bleach marketed as Miracle Mineral Solution could cure the disease caused by the SARS-CoV-2 virus. Trump made similar claims at a press conference in April 2020, proposing that administering bleach by "injection inside or almost a cleaning" could combat the virus. Trump also retweeted many posts by QAnon believers and other conspiracy theorists. It was later discovered that some of these posts came from accounts run by Russian intelligence agents. During the West Coast wildfires in 2020, a former US Senate candidate from Oregon falsely claimed that six members of Antifa had been arrested for starting fires – this was reposted online by Q.

The spread of QAnon

The online message board 4chan was the birthplace of QAnon, where cryptic posts known as "Qdrops" would appear, consisting of alleged intelligence from the highest levels of power. YouTube content creators, 4chan users and Reddit users known as "bakers" spread Q's latest "breadcrumbs" on the internet. In early 2018, the Qdrops moved from 4chan to 8chan (later 8kun). Later in 2018, most active QAnon subforums on Reddit were banned by the site. QAnon subsequently spread to mainstream social media sites. Over 69 million tweets, 487,000 Facebook posts and 281,000 Instagram posts mentioning QAnon were recorded in the period from October 2017 to June 2020. QAnon believers often talked about being "red-pilled", the process by which humans were made aware of reality in the 1999 science fiction film *The Matrix*. QAnon also gained believers around the world in countries including the United Kingdom, Canada, Australia, Germany and Brazil.

Crimes of QAnon

Believers of QAnon soon gained a reputation for trouble and have been involved in various criminal actions:

- In June 2018, believer Matthew Wright blocked traffic with his armoured vehicle on a bridge near the Hoover Dam. Armed to the teeth, he demanded access to a "report" (mentioned in a Qdrop two days earlier) on the FBI agents who had investigated Hillary Clinton's use of a private email server for official communications.

- In March 2019, Anthony Comello shot and killed Gambino crime boss Francesco Cali. He reportedly believed that Cali was a member of the deep state.

- When pro-Trump rioters stormed the Capitol building in January 2021, more than 60 of those arrested were self-identified QAnon believers.

The mysterious Q

On 8 December 2020, a month after Trump's election loss, the final Qdrop was posted online. But who had been behind them? Some QAnon disciples claimed that Q was Trump himself. Other candidates put forward were Trump adviser Steve Bannon, former Trump national security adviser Michael Flynn and/or Republican political operative Roger Stone. Forensic linguists analysed thousands of Qdrops using machine learning and concluded that QAnon was most likely the work of software engineer and 4chan moderator Paul Furber and 8chan/8kun administrator Ron Watkins. It was thought that Furber wrote the earliest Qdrops and helped to enlist the initial "bakers" to spread QAnon beyond 4chan. In 2018 the Qdrops moved to 8chan and it is thought that Watkins became the sole voice of Q. During an interview for the HBO documentary *Q: Into The Storm* (2021), Watkins appeared to admit to writing some of the posts, though he took back the admission almost immediately.

THE PROTOCOLS OF THE ELDERS OF ZION

WHO:
Anti-Semites

WHEN:
1897–present

WHAT:
A document that has been used as "evidence" by conspiracy theorists of a Jewish plot to take over the world

How it began

The Protocols of the Elders of Zion dates back to an alleged meeting of Jewish leaders at the inaugural Zionist Congress in Basel, Switzerland, in 1897. The document was said to be the minutes of that meeting and it was claimed to be evidence of Jewish plans to take over the world and rule it as an autocracy. According to proponents of the theory, the document included instructions on how finance, war and religion can be used as instruments of social and political control, as well as details of the use of brainwashing, suppression, the abuse of authority and the arrest of opponents. The papers were first reproduced in 1903 in Russia, and they continued to appear there in various formats over the next decade or so. Their emergence has been linked to the growing belief at the time that Jews lay behind the country's domestic and foreign woes, particularly the loss of the Russo–Japanese War in 1905.

The spread of an anti-Semitic theory

In the years following the Russian Revolution, frustrated Tsarist exiles continued to spread the theory. These beliefs were further cemented when popular British conspiracy theorist Nesta Webster recycled older Illuminati conspiracy theories, placing new emphasis on the role of Jews in the revolution. In the 1920s and 1930s the *Protocols* were published frequently in the US – by industrialist Henry Ford – and all around Europe, the latter of which was at the time struggling to recover from World War One. Economies on both sides of the Atlantic were heading for depression, and some were keen to blame the Jewish population. From 1933, abridged versions of the document were given to German schoolchildren throughout Nazi Germany, with teachers treating the document as fact. The document was also used by Hitler and his Nazi party as justification for their persecution of Jews.

But wait a minute...

In 1921, Philip Graves published an article in *The Times* (London) demonstrating the obvious resemblance of the *Protocols* to a satire of Napoleon III by the French lawyer Maurice Joly published in 1864: *Dialogue aux enfers entre Machiavel et Montesquieu* ("Dialogue in Hell Between Machiavelli and Montesquieu"). Thanks to further investigation, notably by the Russian historian Vladimir Burtsev, it later emerged that the *Protocols* were forgeries that the Russian secret police had derived from the satirical fantastic novel *Biarritz* by Hermann Goedsche (1868), among other sources. Today, the *Protocols* are widely available in numerous languages, in print and on the Internet. Many anti-Semitic groups still believe that the document is a blueprint for Jewish world domination. It has been described as "probably the most influential work of anti-Semitism ever written".

THE REPTILIAN ELITE

WHO:
The British royal family, world leaders
and anyone else in a position of power

WHEN:
Late twentieth century

WHAT:
Shapeshifting reptilians
are ruling the world

How it began

According to this theory, all those in positions of power and influence – from the British royal family to actors and musicians – are secret shape-shifting reptilians whose one objective is to dominate the human population of Earth. According to some, they have been responsible for all global disasters including 9/11, the Oklahoma City bombing and even the Holocaust. It's not clear when exactly this theory began to take hold, but the concept of reptilian humanoids itself is believed to have emerged from works of fiction by authors such as Robert E. Howard, who wrote about "serpent men" in his story "The Shadow Kingdom", published in *Weird Tales* magazine in August 1929. Historian Edward Guimont has argued that the reptilian conspiracy theory originated with the European colonization of Africa when pseudohistorical legends developed surrounding Great Zimbabwe and the mokele-mbembe, a mythical water-dwelling creature that supposedly lived in the Congo River Basin.

Icke's reptilians

The reptilian elite theory's most outspoken proponent is former footballer and BBC reporter David Icke, who has become renowned for self-publishing books on and speaking about various conspiracy theories, garnering a huge following around the world. In 1999, he published a book called *The Biggest Secret*, in which he claimed, among other things, that the Merovingian dynasty, the Rothschilds, the Bush family, the British royal family and, indeed, most of the world's ancient and modern leaders are blood-drinking, shape-shifting reptilian humanoids involved in a worldwide plot against humanity. The reptilian beings, he states, are part of a race of beings called the Archons, sometimes also called the Anunnaki, who came from the constellation Draco. According to Icke, it is a human/Archon hybrid race of shape-shifting reptilians, known as the "Babylonian Brotherhood", that manipulates global events, keeping humans in constant fear so the Archons can feed off "negative energy".

The hybrid race, Icke claims, first came into being during breeding programmes that took place 200,000–300,000 years ago. The third and latest such programme happened 7,000 years ago, creating the hybrids that currently rule the world. Icke explains that the reptilians come from not only another planet but another dimension – specifically, the lower level of the fourth dimension. This is the dimension nearest the physical world, and from here they control the planet. The only way the hybrid reptilians' influence can be defeated is if people wake up to "the truth", claims Icke. Critics of Icke's theories have pointed out that his introduction of different dimensions allows him to avoid awkward questions about how the reptilians got to Earth. Others have said that Icke's "reptilians" are symbolic representations of Jews and anti-Semitic in nature, which Icke denies.

STRANGE
PHENOMENA

Not many of us can say that we have ever seen an extraterrestrial or a spaceship. But enough people have *claimed* to have seen them to keep the theories about Area 51 and Men in Black in this chapter going for years to come. Likewise, it's not often that you encounter an unidentified big cat out for a stroll in the suburbs of countries such as the UK and Australia. And yet the reported sightings keep coming. When it comes to intriguing archaeological finds such as the Nazca Lines, in the absence of a proven explanation for their existence, the theories abound. But where the notion of a race of people living in the centre of the Earth came from is anybody's guess. Buckle up and enjoy this rollercoaster ride through some of the most "out there" conspiracy theories.

ALIEN BIG CATS

WHO:
Large feline species

WHEN:
1950s–present

WHAT:
People have reported sightings of big cats in places around the world where they don't occur naturally in the wild

How it began

Since the 1950s, members of the public in countries around the world, from Europe to Australia, have been reporting sightings of mysterious large felines in places where they are not native and really wouldn't be expected to be seen. Also known as "phantom cats", these creatures have been spotted on English moors, in Welsh valleys and in the mountains near Sydney. Some have even been captured on camera, their shadowy forms slinking through the undergrowth, often accompanied with a statement by the viewer such as "It was as big as a large dog, but definitely cat-shaped!" These elusive beasts have gripped the public imagination, earning them enigmatic titles such as the Beast of Bodmin Moor, the Blue Mountains Panther and the Tantanoola Tiger. They have become the stuff of urban legend and local folklore. But are big cats really roaming around out there where they shouldn't be, and if they are, then how did they get there?

Big kitty roll call

THE BLUE MOUNTAINS PANTHER

This panther is said to have roamed the mountains near Sydney for over a century. Formal investigations revealed scat and hair samples thought to belong to a big cat, though the official line remained that there wasn't conclusive evidence to prove there was one there.

THE BEAST OF EXMOOR

Big cat sightings began to be reported around Exmoor in the 1970s. In 1983, a local farmer claimed to have lost 100 sheep in the space of three months, all of them killed by throat injuries.

THE GLAWACKUS

Sightings of this terrifying creature, described as a cross between a bear, a panther and a lion, with the screech of a hyena, were reported in 1939 in Glastonbury, Connecticut. Locals claimed that looking into the creature's eyes could wipe your memory.

Where did they come from?

One theory holds that the cats belong to species that have evaded identification for centuries. Evidence has shown that big cats such as lynxes did live in the British Isles at the end of the Ice Age and were supposedly only made extinct locally a few hundred years ago. But what if they weren't rendered obsolete, like the coelacanth, a large fish thought to have died out 66–145 million years ago? Indeed, a live specimen was caught in 1938. In Australia, a creature known as the thylacine, or Tasmanian tiger, once thrived but was made nearly extinct about 2,000 years ago, the final specimens remaining in Tasmania. When the settlers first arrived, there were reports of a strange animal mauling sheep and it was found that the carnivorous marsupial was still there. Unfortunately, by the 1930s, they had been driven to extinction by hunting and habitat destruction. Or had they? Even today, there are still numerous reported sightings.

But wait a minute...

While it seems plausible that an animal could exist unnoticed in the wild expanse of the Australian bush, the chances of a species of large felines remaining undetected in the British countryside seems less likely. So, if the British big cats are real, why haven't they been found? Could it be, as conspiracists have suggested, that the government is suppressing evidence of their existence to conserve them, because if word got out about them, they would be hunted to extinction by trophy seekers? It seems more likely that any actual big cats roaming around are escaped animals from private collections or pets abandoned by their owners. Many of the sightings are also probably cases of mistaken identity when viewing animals at distance and with compromised visibility. But maybe it's best not to go wandering out there alone in the dark. Just in case.

AREA 51

WHO:
The US government

WHEN:
1955–present

WHAT:
Secret activities take place at a
maximum-security military airfield
in the Nevada desert, where some
believe alien spacecraft are stored

How it began

In 1955, a former airfield in a remote part of the Nevada desert near Roswell, New Mexico was turned into a top-secret site known as Area 51, a name that wasn't recognized by the US government until 2013. Back then, the US government claimed to be using it to develop spy planes, but that has now finished and any spy planes have been moved from the area. It is not known what goes on there today. But whatever is happening is shrouded in secrecy and plagued by rumours of weird goings-on. The large airbase is not recorded on any map. We know it's there because some members of the public have managed to photograph it from nearby hills. There are also pictures that were taken by Russian and commercial satellites, some of which show a recently built hangar. This suggests that, whatever the government have been up to there, they are still very much getting up to it.

Maximum security

Area 51 is sectioned off by a strict no-fly zone that extends all the way up to space. The whole zone is fenced off and monitored by hundreds of closed-circuit security cameras. There is a heavy military presence at the base, and the personnel go to excessive measures to stop anyone entering. Signs warn would-be intruders that deadly force and violence may very likely be used against anyone attempting to enter without authorization. Camouflaged vehicles bearing government plates, manned by men in military-style desert uniforms armed with M16 rifles patrol the roads surrounding the area, roads which are full of sensors that alert the base to any vehicle movement. If Area 51 is a military firing range, it would make sense to keep people out for their own safety. And yet, the security measures seem in excess of what would be required by a conventional military base. Someone seems very keen to keep people out.

What's really going on there?

Officially, Area 51 is a military testing facility. But given the amount of secrecy surrounding the base, it's hardly surprising there are conspiracy theories about it. One such hypothesis says Area 51 is a UFO research centre. Conspiracists point to the infamous incident at Roswell in 1947, when the wreckage of what was believed at the time to be a flying saucer was removed from a ranch in New Mexico. Maybe the wreckage was taken to Area 51 for further investigation and has stayed there ever since. Maybe there were even extraterrestrials found in the wreckage and transported to the base for further studies. And could scientists at the base be working to understand and recreate the alien technology they captured? Had aliens succeeded in reaching Earth, their technology would be far superior to our own and would be worth examining for ways in which it could be exploited to give the US the technological edge over rival nations.

Storm Area 51

In June 2019, Matty Roberts posted an event on Facebook called "Storm Area 51, They Can't Stop All of Us", inviting users to join him in Area 51 to search for extraterrestrials. More than 2 million people responded "going" and 1.5 million clicked "interested". Two music festivals called Alienstock and Storm Area 51 Basecamp were planned in towns nearby the base to coincide with the event. On the day of the event in September 2019, only about 150 people turned up at the two entrances to Area 51. None succeeded in entering the site. It is just as well that they didn't. Early that year, on 28 January, an unidentified man drove through a security checkpoint towards the base. An 8-mile vehicle pursuit ensued. The man eventually got out of his vehicle carrying a "cylindrical object" and did not obey requests by security officers to halt. He was shot dead.

THE NAZCA LINES

WHO:
The Nazca people

WHEN:
Between 500 BCE and 500 CE

WHAT:
Mysterious lines carved into the Nazca Desert have been the subject of much speculation about their origin

What are they?

On a high plateau in the Peruvian Andes, 250 miles south of Lima, thousands of mysterious lines adorn the dry surface of the Nazca Desert. The strange markings bear a likeness to drawings of simple geometric patterns, shapes and straight lines, as well as more complicated shapes such as birds, spiders, lizards, apes, fish and other unidentifiable animals. They are best viewed from the air, as many of the forms are indistinguishable from close-up on the ground. Which begs the question: since the ancient Nazca had no known method of flying, how and why did they create them? Carbon-dating technology has estimated their origin at around 1,500 years ago. In the years leading up to 2020, between 80 and 100 new figures were discovered with the use of drones. Archaeologists believe that yet more are waiting to be found.

Visitors from afar

What if the lines weren't created by the Nazca people at all? What if, in fact, visiting aliens constructed them? In 1968, Erich von Däniken published a book entitled *Chariot of the Gods: Unsolved Mysteries of the Past* which suggested exactly that. According to his speculations, the lines were a landing strip for alien spaceships. He also claimed that these visiting extraterrestrials constructed other wonders such as the pyramids of Giza. In their book, *The Morning of the Magicians*, Louis Pauwels and Jacques Bergier proposed that aliens had visited Earth many thousands of years ago, during human prehistory, and were involved in creating the lines. This alien species possessed highly advanced technology and intelligence and helped primeval human beings to gain superiority over other species and take over the planet.

Secret meetings

The idea that the markings may have been made by or have something to do with aliens has persisted. One theory posits that the marks were created by humans with the intention of attracting aliens to Earth. Some, who believe that the aliens themselves made the markings, believe the aliens visited Earth to carry out a secret meeting with world leaders. Using the otherwise deserted area to land their enormous craft, the alien emissaries then travelled in secret to meet with the leaders and returned to the same remote spot to leave. According to those who believe this theory, the extraterrestrials return to Earth regularly for such meetings and that is why the lines haven't been erased. Rather, they are fresh marks from recent landings – the theorists point to the lines newly discovered in the late 2010s to support this theory.

But wait a minute...

Aliens landing on Earth may seem an unlikely solution to this ancient puzzle. And yet, none of the theories put forward by various researchers and scientists have proved conclusive, either. These have included:

- Paul Kosok, a US scholar who held that the lines were created to align with the stars.
- Archaeologist Johan Reinhard theorized that the lines were part of religious practices involving the worship of deities associated with the availability of water.
- Swiss art historian Henri Stierlin proposed that the lines were used as giant, primitive looms to create extremely long strings and wide pieces of textile.

Whatever the truth may be, the Nazca Lines seem set to fascinate and mystify us for years to come.

MEN IN BLACK

WHO:
Men dressed in black

WHEN:
c. 1947–present

WHAT:
People who claim to have been visited
by extraterrestrials say that they
are subsequently interrogated and/
or terrorized by these individuals

Sinister figures

As if coming face to face with extraterrestrials isn't terrifying enough, individuals who have had such encounters have also reported later being visited by sinister men dressed in black suits. The Men in Black (MIB) are said to have interrogated, harassed and threatened these individuals, and it's been claimed that they have wiped their victims' memories and even assassinated them. They tend to travel in pairs in either black cars or black helicopters. Witnesses have described them as unusually tall, and some have no fingernails. They speak with a strange accent that doesn't come from any known country on Earth and seem to be able to do so without moving their lips. Their identity is a secret and they are clearly prepared to go to any lengths needed to keep it that way.

How it began

The first reference to MIB may date back to an incident that occurred on 27 June 1947. Harold Dahl was out on his boat near Washington State's Maury Island undertaking conservation work when he saw six doughnut-shaped aircraft hovering about half a mile overhead. One of them fell nearly 1,500 feet, raining debris down on the boat. Dahl took pictures of the aircraft, which he later showed to his supervisor, Fred Crisman. Crisman himself visited the scene and saw a strange aircraft. Dahl claimed that the next day he was visited by a man in a black suit who could recount in extraordinary detail what Dahl had just experienced. He told Dahl never to speak of the incident. If he did, bad things would happen. The Maury Island incident was later deemed a hoax, but the spectre of the MIB had already lodged in the public imagination.

The case of
Shirley Greenfield

In her book, *Men in Black: Investigating the Truth Behind the Phenomenon*, Jenny Randles recounts the case of Shirley Greenfield, the victim of an alien abduction. According to Randles, two men appeared at the Greenfields' home nine days after the abduction and demanded to speak with Shirley. They addressed each other only as "commander" and refused to say where they were from. They grilled Shirley about her abduction and ended the conversation with a strict warning that she must not relay it to anyone. Shirley had been reluctant to tell them about some physical marks left on her upper arms after the abduction. Over the next week, she was plagued by telephone calls from the "commander", who kept asking her if she had physical evidence of what had happened. When she finally confessed that she did have physical marks, the interrogator seemed relieved, and the telephone calls stopped.

Who are they?

To date, no one has been able to come up with a satisfactory answer to who the mysterious **MIB** are, but it hasn't stopped people trying. Here are just some of the ideas that have been advanced:

- They are part of a government conspiracy to silence the victims of UFO activity. Such activity has unearthed an extra dimension of the universe that the government is anxious for no one to find out about.

- The MIB are part of a government conspiracy with an extraterrestrial race to abduct humans for medical experiments in exchange for technological know-how.

- They have nothing to do with the government or extraterrestrials and represent an organization or power about which we are unaware.

HOLLOW EARTH

WHO:
Various thinkers throughout history

WHEN:
Late seventeenth century–present

WHAT:
The Earth is hollow and a secret race of people lives at the centre

How it began

People have been discussing the concept that the Earth is hollow and contains a substantial interior space since as far back as the late seventeenth century, when Edmond Halley put it forward as a hypothesis. According to the theories that circulate today, not only is the Earth hollow but its interior space is inhabited by a strange race of people (perhaps descendants of survivors from the Atlantis culture). Supporters of this thesis claim that there is a sun in the centre of the hollow, which is smaller than our own sun but large enough to give light and warmth. Conspiracists use this to explain the aurora borealis or aurora australis in evidence often seen near the Earth's two poles. These are said to be the sites of two secret entrances, of which there are several strategically placed around the globe and from which flying saucers periodically emerge.

The theories

There are numerous variations on this theory, some of which are summarized here:

- 🛸 The Nazis discovered an entrance into this secret world just before the collapse of the Third Reich and built a secret base inside. They are waiting for an opportune moment to relaunch their campaign against the outer Earth.

- 🛸 The inhabitants of the interior of Earth are not physical in nature and our normal earthly matter is no barrier to them.

- 🛸 The inhabitants are four-dimensional beings. The extra dimension is incomprehensible to humans but allows these bizarre beings to communicate telepathically with us.

- 🛸 There are underground cities in the interior built by aliens that use the centre of Earth as a base.

How to journey to the centre of the Earth

If there really is an interior space inside the Earth, how does one get in there? That remains a mystery. Some claim that Earth is shaped like a doughnut, with two holes at each pole providing an entrance. Others say there is one entrance accessed through tunnels, caves and potholes. Then again, the entrances could be hidden inside Area 51 and other mysterious regions of the world. Many agree that if there is an entrance to the centre of Earth, this giant hole must have been concealed with the use of advanced technology – perhaps through the use of holograms, mind control or other psychological means, time travel or by methods that we cannot even imagine.

But wait a minute...

Since Edmond Halley first proposed his hypothesis about the Earth being hollow back in the seventeenth century, there have been numerous counter-arguments to his ideas:

- An expedition to the Chimborazo volcano in Ecuador in 1735 and a subsequent one to the Schiehallion mountain in 1772 used a vertical deflection experiment at two different altitudes to determine how local mass anomalies affected gravitational pull and therefore disprove the hollow Earth theory.

- Study of seismic activity based on the time it takes the waves to travel through and around the Earth indicates the planet is mostly filled with solid rock, liquid nickel-iron alloy and solid nickel-iron.

- The small matter of gravity. A hollow planet with a shell the thickness of the Earth's crust would not withstand the gravity acting upon it and would implode.

HEALTH AND TECHNOLOGY

Mistrust of technology and the pharmaceutical industry is nothing new. There are conspiracy theories about "Big Pharma" and surveillance stretching back as far as these things have been around. Since the Covid-19 pandemic began, the paranoia has gone up a gear, with the early 2020s seeing a massive resurgence of theories about public health and technology. At the time of writing, the origin of the SARS-CoV-2 virus that causes the disease Covid-19 has not been definitively identified, leading to many a speculation about cover-ups and even the virus being deliberately created. Meanwhile, the Covid-19 vaccination drive added fuel to the fire of anti-vaccination campaigners. And who knows what world governments are planning by creating digital currencies, so the conspiracists warn, but as those folks will tell you, it can be nothing good. Just make sure no one microchips you, because then it will surely be game over.

BIG PHARMA IS CONNING US

WHO:

The world's leading
pharmaceutical companies

WHEN:

The era of modern medicine

WHAT:

The big pharmaceutical companies
are covering up affordable and natural
health remedies so that they can make
profit from their own health products

What is the theory?

Pharmaceutical companies play a vital role in supplying the world's population with medicines and treatments. But some believe that these companies are involved in sinister activities: namely, the suppression of natural remedies and less costly drugs so that they can continue to make a profit from their own health products. Some conspiracy theorists even claim that the drug industry controls every healthcare system in the world and deliberately withholds cures for cancer, diabetes, HIV and several other infectious diseases because the availability of these cures would damage Big Pharma's profits. And worse: it is claimed that drug companies ensure high incidence of the diseases that their drugs treat and even generate new strains of these diseases. For example, there were allegations that a US drug company "accidentally" released a contaminated batch of H1N1 flu virus treatments which were capable of spreading the virus.

The plot thickens

Some conspiracists claim that it is not just capitalist greed that motivates Big Pharma in their nefarious doings – it is also part of a sinister plan for global domination. According to proponents of this theory, those who are running the world's major drug companies also belong to a clandestine cabal whose goal is to install a One World Government, an authoritarian, fascist state. The population will then be subservient to the needs of the master race. So where does Big Pharma come into it? By perpetuating debilitating and deadly diseases, the drugs industry can make enough money to finance this future revolution, so the suspicious believe. The prevalence of these illnesses is also a means of keeping the general populace de-radicalized and enslaved.

Case study: the HIV/AIDS epidemic

Various theories have circulated regarding the AIDS virus. One holds that antiretroviral drugs are toxins disseminated by doctors who have been corrupted by the pharmaceutical industry. Journalist Celia Farber wrote in a 2006 column for *Harper's Magazine* that the antiretroviral drug nevirapine was part of a conspiracy by the "scientific-medical complex" to spread toxic drugs. She claimed that nevirapine had been administered to pregnant women in clinical trials, leading to a fatality, and that AIDS is not caused by HIV. Farber's assertions were strongly refuted by scientists, but the damage had already been done, with the resulting publicity acting as a catalyst for AIDS denialism. The former President of South Africa, Thabo Mbeki, was influenced by AIDS denier Peter Duesberg. According to estimates, more than 300,000 people died prematurely as a result of the president's policies, which prevented AIDS patients from receiving the proper treatments.

But wait a minute...

There are some level-headed arguments as to why the drug industry might not be as sinister as people think:

 Conspiracists often claim that pharmaceutical companies financially pressure researchers and journals into suppressing negative research about their drugs. And yet top journals regularly publish papers critical of specific drugs.

 Steven Novella, clinical neurologist and host of *The Skeptics' Guide to the Universe* podcast, has commented that, while the pharmaceutical industry has aspects that deserve criticism, by demonizing and attacking the industry theorists are actually letting it "off the hook" by distracting from more considered criticisms.

 In 2016, science writer David Robert Grimes published a research paper that estimated that if Big Pharma did conceal a cure for cancer, it would only remain concealed for about 3.2 years because of the huge number of people required to keep it secret.

MICROCHIP IMPLANTS

WHO:

Religious groups

WHEN:

Early 2000s

WHAT:

Microchip implants are the mark of the
beast and will be used to control us

How it began

In the early 2000s, the chip and PIN method of payment was rolled out across the world. For many conspiracy theorists, this signalled the coming of dark times indeed. According to them, in the future much smaller chips would be manufactured and implanted in people's bodies, and then used to manipulate them. In this dystopian image of the future, we would no longer need to use PINs or even passports, because all information about us would be stored in a chip the size of a grain of rice embedded in our hands which could be read or traced through walls and over great distances. And, while it hasn't been implemented worldwide just yet, it wasn't long before such a technology itself became a reality: in 2017, biometric chips were implanted into dozens of employees of Three Square Market, a Wisconsin-based company specializing in vending machines.

A prophecy fulfilled

Religious groups have had a thing or two to say about the potential rollout of a microchip implant programme. For them, it would be the fulfilment of an ominous prophecy made a long time ago:

> *And he causeth all, both small and great, rich and poor, free and bond, to receive a mark in their right hand, or in their foreheads: And that no man might buy or sell, save he that had the mark, or the name of the beast, or the number of his name. Here is wisdom. Let him that hath understanding count the number of the beast: for it is the number of a man; and his number is 666.*
> **Revelation 13:16–18**

Tim Willard, the managing director of US magazine *The Futurist*, has stated that everyone's social security number will consist of "a new, global, 18-digit mesh block configuration of international numbers that will allow people to be tracked internationally". And the format that number will take? Three sets of six: 6-6-6.

The rollout has already begun

Some proponents of this theory believe that with the coming of the mark of the beast there will be a single world government, divided into ten nations. One of these "nations", the European Union, has already been formed, with a single currency in most of its participating countries. But what if people reject this "mark"? It is thought that only those who accept the chips will have a place in the soon-to-be-established new society. In fact, it is likely that the microchips will be made compulsory for identification purposes. Some believe this process has already started, and that the government has been secretly injecting chips into people having routine medical procedures. It is true that chips have already been developed for some groups of vulnerable people considered at risk of straying from safety – for example, autism sufferers and people with Alzheimer's. Maybe it is only a matter of time before mass-chipping becomes reality?

ELECTRONIC BANKING

WHO:

The world's banks and governments
and the shadowy cabal seeking to
set up the New World Order

WHEN:

Present

WHAT:

Electronic banking is being used as
a means of controlling the masses

What is the theory?

According to conspiracy theorists, a shadowy cabal is plotting to establish a New World Order (see page 10). Sometimes linked to the Illuminati, the objective of this secretive super-organization is to rule the world and ensure that whatever happens benefits its members. And what better way to master the masses than by taking control of their finances through electronic banking? The preparations and early phases of this plan are said to have been happening as far back as antiquity. If you want a taste of how it all might work in practice, you need only consult Margaret Atwood's dystopian novel *The Handmaid's Tale*, in which women's bank accounts and credit cards are frozen, allowing the new dictatorial regime to dominate their lives. Or you could watch the sci-fi series *Revolution*, in which a worldwide blackout strips everyone of their wealth and causes the breakdown of social order.

Step by step to dystopia

Proponents of this theory trace the process back to the Renaissance, when currency based on precious metals in coin form was replaced with paper notes. In phase two, virtual money – in the form of credit cards with numerical data encoded on a magnetic strip – replaced tangible currency. Phase three ushered in the advent of e-commerce, with many websites no longer even requiring credit cards to buy and sell over the internet. Phase four relates to the restructuring of worldwide banking, with large international conglomerate banks putting power into the hands of the few and making it easier for finances to be controlled. Next, the theorists claim, would come the worldwide implementation of an electronic identity card. And finally, a huge disaster will be engineered, causing a worldwide blackout à la *Revolution*, destroying all data and electronic accounts. The population will be left with nothing, and the New World Order will rise up and control the poverty-stricken world.

Central bank digital currencies

In a world where many of the world's leading economies are now considering introducing central bank digital currencies (CBDCs), it may appear that we are not too far off this dystopian vision of the future. The exact nature of CBDCs varies from country to country, but essentially the concept is of a digital version of physical cash, with the money being issued by the central bank (rather than being created by private entities, as is the case with cryptocurrencies).

The Coutts financial scandal (in which former Brexit Party leader Nigel Farage's bank accounts were closed by the private bank) and the Silicon Valley Bank collapse have been pointed to by conspiracy theorists as further justification for their claims.

Since governments including the UK and EU have set up task forces to work on the creation of CBDCs, the internet has been awash with conspiracy theories about what that might mean for regular people. Beliefs about CBDCs include:

- The Covid-19 pandemic was planned in order to subdue the global population and CBDCs will now be used to further manipulate it.
- If banks switch to CBDCs, mortgage contracts could be voided.
- CBDCs will allow the state to restrict what people can buy. For example, limits could be placed on meat and fuel consumption as a way of reducing obesity or combating climate change, and some sectors of society could be prevented from buying guns.

ANTI-VACCINATION

WHO:
Members of the public

WHEN:
Since vaccinations were first invented,
but particularly since the 1990s

WHAT:
Vaccinations are not to be trusted as they
have various undesirable side effects
and are part of a huge cover-up

How it began

Opposition to vaccination has existed for centuries, probably ever since Edward Jenner first began immunizing people against smallpox back in the late eighteenth century. Since then, scientists have developed vaccines to prevent and reduce the severity of multiple diseases, saving the lives and safeguarding the health of millions of people. Most of humanity accepts that childhood vaccinations are a necessary part of growing up in order to help children live a longer, healthier life. But since the rise of the internet and social media, the intentional spread of vaccine-related misinformation has led to an increasing number of people resisting vaccination – for their children and themselves. Conspiracists believe that something sinister is afoot, and that a cover-up of huge proportions lies behind the systematic vaccination of children. With the roll-out of the Covid-19 vaccination starting in 2020, yet more misinformation and conspiracy theories have surfaced.

Vaccines can cause autism in children

In the late 1990s, suspicions began to arise in anti-vaccination camps that vaccines may be causing autism in children. Controversy was focused in particular around the MMR vaccine, which is given to every child in the UK aged 12-15 months. In 1998, a scientific paper published in *The Lancet* by Andrew Wakefield argued that MMR could cause childhood autism. From 2001 onward this was discredited, with Wakefield himself eventually admitting that it was not based on solid evidence. And yet the belief has persisted, with many claiming that Big Pharma discredited Wakefield because they didn't want to lose out on profits if the dangerous truth about vaccination was uncovered. Donald Trump has added to this, repeatedly saying that vaccines can cause autism in children. Multiple large-scale scientific studies of more than half a million children have found that there is no link.

Bill Gates is microchipping us all

When the rollout of Covid-19 vaccinations began in late 2020, it wasn't long before the conspiracy theories began to roll out too. At the centre of one of the most prominent theories was Bill Gates, co-founder of the company Microsoft. And just what might this tech giant have to do with vaccination of the masses? The theorists believed that Gates was behind a massive scheme to implant trackable microchips into all of us, and the Covid-19 pandemic itself was just one big smokescreen to allow him to put his plans into action by injecting the chips along with the Covid vaccine. Polls taken at the time suggested that 28 per cent of Americans believed in this conspiracy theory. In fact, in an interview in March 2020, Gates did state his belief that eventually there would be digital certificates to show who'd recovered, been tested and received a vaccine, but he never made any mention of microchips.

Other vaccine myths busted

Many other myths and conspiracy theories about vaccines have circulated, for example:

- Vaccines cause infertility: In 2020, as the Covid-19 vaccination was distributed, fears arose that the mRNA vaccine-induced antibodies which act against the SARS-CoV-2 spike protein could also attack the placental protein syncytin-1, causing infertility. There is no evidence to support this.

- Vaccines can cause the disease that they vaccinate against: This is not possible with traditional vaccines because the virus is attenuated (weakened). In newer types of vaccines such as mRNA, the vaccine does not contain the virus at all.

- Vaccines can cause harmful side effects and death: In reality, vaccines are very safe. Any side effects are usually mild and temporary, such as a sore throat or mild fever, which can be controlled by taking paracetamol.

COVID-19

WHO:
All manner of nefarious and secretive
individuals or organizations

WHEN:
2020–present

WHAT:
There are various theories
about the origins of the virus that
caused the Covid-19 pandemic

How it began

In November 2019, a new strain of coronavirus named SARS-CoV-2 was first identified. The novel virus caused the disease Covid-19 and its emergence triggered a global pandemic – as well as a spate of conspiracy theories about its origins. The initial outbreak was linked to a "wet market" in Wuhan, China, where caged live animals were held for sale. Scientists proposed that the virus had made the jump there from animals to humans – they believed that bats were the original reservoir, though the virus may have transitioned via an intermediary species. Claims began to surface that the Chinese government had tried to cover up the outbreak, or at least be economical about its scale. The persecution of doctors in China who tried to warn about the disease was widely reported in media at the time. In March 2020, a Chinese government spokesman infamously tweeted: "It might be [the] US Army who brought the epidemic to Wuhan."

Wuhan lab theory

As the outbreak spread, causing millions of deaths around the world, a sinister theory began to circulate: that the virus was created deliberately. Proponents of this theory pointed to the fact that the Institute of Virology, which houses China's only level-four biosafety laboratory (the highest classification of labs that study deadly viruses), is situated in Wuhan. The hypothesis is that scientists in the laboratory were trying to devise an all-purpose vaccine and they created SARS-CoV-2 to give the vaccine something to work against. A dozen lab staff were accidentally infected and the unit was sealed, but one person escaped and spread the disease all over the city. It is alleged the Chinese government invented the wet market story as a cover-up. Worse, some believe that the virus was created as a bioweapon and intentionally released. The lab leak theory has been widely renounced by scientists and credited with kindling anti-China sentiment.

5G

The emergence of the SARS-CoV-2 virus coincided with the switch-on of the 5G network in China, a fact that did not escape the attention of conspiracy theorists, who were already suspicious that the mobile technology would cause negative health effects. The link between 5G and Covid-19 gained traction after American singer Keri Hilson tweeted: "People have been trying to warn us about 5G for YEARS. Petitions, organizations, studies… what we're going through is the affects [*sic*] of radiation. 5G launched in CHINA. Nov 1, 2019. People dropped dead." Around that time videos of people "dropping on the ground and fainting" in China went viral, which conspiracy theorists claimed was caused by 5G radio waves interfering with the oxygen levels in the victims' blood. Other theorists believed that the Covid-19 vaccine would be used to implant microchips in the population (see page 68), and that the chips would be controlled by 5G.

We were warned...

What's worse than being hit by a deadly pandemic? Knowing that it was coming and doing nothing about it. Some conspiracy theorists claim this is exactly what happened. The warnings were right before our eyes, they say: in an episode of *The Simpsons*. A Facebook post showing stills from a 1993 episode went viral. They showed Homer Simpson and Principal Skinner being infected by a virus, and a news anchor reading from a piece of paper while the words "corona virus" and a cat appeared on a screen behind him. However, it later emerged that the images had been doctored and the text behind the news anchor actually read "Apocalypse Meow". But what about the 1981 book *The Eyes of Darkness* by Dean Koontz, in which a boy is held captive in Wuhan, China, the site of a deadly virus outbreak with very similar symptoms to Covid-19? One passage gave details of a virus called "Wuhan-400", developed at a lab outside the city.

LEGENDARY

This, the final chapter, will explore world-famous conspiracy theories that have captured the public's imagination and become iconic. Let's face it: no self-respecting anthology of conspiracy theories could omit the one about the Moon landings being faked, a feat that would be hugely impressive, if it had really happened. Two well-known deceased public figures – John F. Kennedy and Elvis Presley – are featured here, with conjectures about why one of them was killed and why one of them is still alive. You will also encounter the "flat Earthers", those wonderful folk who will merrily tell you that the Earth is not, in fact, round but flat. There is reference to a darker chapter in world history too, with a section on the chilling theories surrounding the 9/11 terrorist attacks. And then there is that persistent rumour about how chemtrails are being used to manipulate the population…

THE NASA MOON LANDING HOAX

WHO:
NASA and the US government

WHEN:
1969

WHAT:
The televised first Moon
landing mission was faked

How it began

On 20 July 1969, 650 million people around the world sat glued to their television sets as Neil Armstrong stepped out of the Apollo 11 lunar module and onto the surface of the Moon in "one giant leap for mankind". Or did he? According to conspiracists, NASA and the US government faked the whole thing – it was all filmed on a set on Earth. Even as the Moon landing was happening, some people were already questioning whether it could be real, but the suspicions really gained ground in the early to mid-1970s. In 1976, Bill Kaysing self-published a pamphlet titled "We Never Went to the Moon: America's Thirty Billion Dollar Swindle", and in 1978 the movie *Capricorn One* portrayed a faked landing on Mars. The theory has taken root in popular culture ever since, with the 2018 reboot of *The X-Files* and many other fictional TV shows such as *Futurama* and *Friends* revisiting it over the years.

The foundations of a lie

But why would the US government embark on such a project? The 1960s had seen the US engaged in a heated Space Race with their Cold War enemy, the Soviet Union, to be the first nation to put a man on the Moon. President John F. Kennedy had even promised in a 1961 speech that the US would do it "before this decade is out". Failure was not an option: it would have been deeply humiliating and undermined the US at a time when the two superpowers were competing for influence in a world increasingly divided between capitalism and communism. And so, the theory goes, the US government created Moon-like sets and manufactured the iconic footage, purportedly with the aid of filmmaker Stanley Kubrick, who had recently created rather convincing moonscape footage for his sci-fi epic *2001: A Space Odyssey*.

The clues

In 1972, NASA abruptly ceased its Moon landings programme. Suspicious, perhaps? But not quite so suspicious as anomalies revealed by scrutiny of photographs and footage from the Apollo 11 mission:

- None of the photographs have stars in them. Perhaps because their position would have revealed that the photos were in fact taken on Earth?

- There is inconsistency in the angle and colour of the shadows. Was this due to the use of artificial lights?

- Several photos that have captions saying they were taken miles apart have identical backgrounds. Could a painted backdrop have been used?

- Photographs show a rock on the ground with two matching C's on it. Was this a labelled studio prop?

- In film footage of Buzz Aldrin planting an American flag, the flag is clearly fluttering in a breeze – which would be impossible in the vacuum of space.

But wait a minute...

The evidence amassed by the theorists is certainly extensive. But what about the hundreds of Moon rocks that have been examined by scientists around the world and confirmed to be of extraterrestrial origin? How would NASA have acquired them without going to the Moon? How to explain the presence of the gear left behind by astronauts and trails made by the Apollo landing equipment that was recorded by NASA's Lunar Reconnaissance Orbiter in 2011? And how could it be possible for the 400,000+ people who worked on the Apollo project for nearly ten years – astronauts, pilots, scientists, engineers, technicians and skilled labourers – to have kept such a whopping great secret? If they had pulled it off, it would be extraordinary. Maybe that's why this conspiracy theory holds enduring appeal to this day.

THE EARTH IS FLAT

WHO:

Flat Earthers

WHEN:

Late nineteenth century–present

WHAT:

Holders of the theory believe that the
Earth is flat rather than spherical

How it began

Our ancient predecessors believed the Earth was flat. It wasn't until Eratosthenes measured the Earth's circumference in 240 BCE and, much later, in 1519-22 CE, Portuguese explorers circumnavigated the Earth, that most people became convinced that the Earth is a globe shape. In the late nineteenth century, the flat Earth concept resurfaced when English writer Samuel Rowbotham (1816-84) published a pamphlet called "Zetetic Astronomy", in which he claimed that the Earth is a plane or disc with the North Pole at its centre, ringed by a wall of ice, and that the Sun, Moon, planets and stars move only several hundred miles above the Earth's surface. After he died, Lady Elizabeth Blount established a Universal Zetetic Society to propagate his ideas. This was succeeded in 1956 by Samuel Shenton's International Flat Earth Research Society, which has continued in various formats to this day.

The round Earth conspiracy

Those who believe the Earth is flat call themselves "Flat Earthers". They believe that the true nature of our planet's shape is being covered up by NASA and other government agencies. What of all those satellite photos that show the Earth as a globe? The images are fakes, photoshopped by NASA, so the conspiracists aver. Airline pilots are tricked into thinking that they are flying around the world because all aeroplane GPS devices have been rigged to hide the truth – that the planes are travelling around in circles above our disc-shaped habitat. But why would NASA and the government go to such a huge effort to keep Earth's flatness a secret? According to The Flat Earth Society, their motivation is financial. Those in on the conspiracy benefit from the funding the government puts into NASA and other space agencies, and the cost of faking a space programme is much lower than actually having one.

The school of Flat Earth

Flat Earthers' concepts about how the world works extend beyond the question of the planet's pancake dimensions. Ever distrusting of the scientific community, they have reassessed many things taught in schools and developed the following alternative teachings:

- According to Flat Earth geography, the Arctic Circle sits at the centre of the Earth disc. Antarctica, on the other hand, is a 150-foot-tall wall of ice that sits around the rim. Those helpful folk at NASA guard the ice wall and prevent people from climbing up and falling over the edge.

- Flat Earth astronomy teaches us that while the Earth is flat, the Sun is a sphere 32 miles (51 km) in diameter. It moves in circles 3,000 miles (4,828 km) above the plane of the Earth, illuminating the different time zone sections of the planet in a 24-hour cycle and causing night and day to happen.

The Moon is also a sphere, the same size as the sun, and there is an invisible "anti-Moon" that sometimes moves in front of the Moon, causing lunar eclipses. Stars are spherical objects moving in a plane thousands of miles above the surface of the Earth.

Flat Earth physicists hold that the force of "gravity" scientists have perceived at play on Earth is an illusion. Rather than accelerating downward, falling objects are met by the Earth disc accelerating upward at 32 feet per second squared (9.8 metres per second squared), driven by a force named "dark energy".

THE ASSASSINATION OF JOHN F. KENNEDY

WHO:

John F. Kennedy

WHEN:

1963–present

WHAT:

President Kennedy was assassinated
as part of a wider conspiracy theory

How it began

On 22 November 1963, President John F. Kennedy was riding in a presidential motorcade through Dealey Plaza in Dallas, Texas when he was fatally shot by former US Marine Lee Harvey Oswald. Kennedy was rushed to Parkland Memorial Hospital, where he was pronounced dead about 30 minutes after the shooting. Shortly after assassinating Kennedy, Oswald gunned down Dallas policeman J. D. Tippit. Around 70 minutes later, Oswald was apprehended by the Dallas Police Department and charged with the murders of Kennedy and Tippit. On 24 November 1963, Oswald himself was fatally shot by Dallas nightclub operator Jack Ruby. In the aftermath of the shootings, conspiracy theories as to who may have arranged the killing of JFK – and then had Oswald shot to keep him quiet – began to proliferate. Despite the official investigation ruling that Oswald acted alone and not as part of a conspiracy, these theories only continued to gain momentum and are still going today.

The work of the Mafia?

It was not widely known at the time, but JFK's brother, Robert, had been combating organized crime in the US. Mafia gang members had allegedly said that it would be good to get rid of either Robert or JFK. Assassinating the president would certainly act as a clear warning to the US government to stop meddling in their affairs. Witnesses had claimed to have seen Oswald with Mafia gang members on several occasions. If Oswald had been working for the Mafia, it would make sense for them to hire someone else – i.e. Jack Ruby – to kill Oswald to stop him revealing the truth. The Mafia also had reasons for stopping JFK's plans to pull out of the Vietnam War, so theorists claim. Gangsters were making a lot of money off drugs smuggled out of the country, and the US military presence in the country indirectly prevented the Vietnamese authorities from tackling this.

A CIA killing?

Relations between JFK and the CIA had soured considerably after the Bay of Pigs debacle, in which Cuban exiles aided by sponsorship and training from the CIA invaded Cuba to overthrow Fidel Castro's government. The operation was a failure for which the president and the CIA blamed each other. Perhaps, the conspiracists claim, Kennedy had also discovered a plot against either him personally or the government and the CIA decided to silence him before he could say anything. If this was the case, the CIA would want to leave no trace behind. Hiring an outside assassin like Oswald who was unprofessional would help them to cover their tracks. And maybe Oswald was merely the gunman that the public was meant to see. Maybe, the theory goes, there was also a second gunman, a professional CIA-trained sniper, hiding inside the grassy knoll from where the deadly shot was fired.

A military-industrial complex masterplan?

The Mafia were not the only ones disgruntled by Kennedy's plans to pull out of Vietnam. It also ruffled feathers among the military-industrial complex, the "Iron Triangle" of the government, armed forces and the manufacturing industries. Heads of industry were already angry over JFK's handling of Cuba. Kennedy had issued a statement saying that once the 1964 presidential election was over, he would pull troops out of Vietnam. His re-election was all but certain. But of course, he never got the chance. Four days after the assassination, President Lyndon B. Johnson, who succeeded Kennedy, sent more troops into Vietnam, which no doubt delighted the Mafia and the military-industrial complex. But where would the FBI have come into all of this? Most likely they would have been co-conspirators, rather than assassins; it is possible that they would have had some prior intelligence of a murder planned by the military-industrial complex.

A government plot?

The motive given for the US government wanting JFK gone is not perhaps what you might expect. It had been 16 years since the Roswell incident, when mysterious debris thought to have come from an alien spaceship crashed to Earth. The government had remained cryptic about the truth of that day's events. Whatever extraterrestrial secrets they may have been hiding, they probably wouldn't have been keen for the public to learn that they were the result of space travel. Especially not if, as the theory goes, the government had made a secret deal with the aliens that they could abduct humans and test them in return for advanced technology – a deal which some believe Kennedy had found out about, along with the government's other secret space missions and the base they were building on the Moon to house up to 40,000 humans. Rather than give him the chance to go public about this information, they had him murdered.

But wait a minute...

Most conspiracy theorists were not convinced when the ten-month Warren Commission investigation concluded in September 1964 that the president was shot by Lee Harvey Oswald, who was murdered before he could stand trial. However, there are many factors that suggest Oswald did indeed act alone. If there was a conspiracy, then the following questions would be raised:

- How could the conspirators have produced such a huge volume of evidence against Oswald in such a short space of time, with only a few days to make their plans after the announcement of the parade route?

- Why would it have taken place in such a public location? If the CIA or the FBI was behind it, surely they would have used a more sophisticated and subtle method?

- Why would the CIA, FBI, Mafia or military-industrial complex choose Oswald as assassin, rather than the many expert gunmen they had to choose from?

ELVIS PRESLEY

WHO:

Elvis Presley

WHEN:

1977–present

WHAT:

There are numerous conspiracy
theories surrounding the performer,
including that he faked his own
death and is in fact still alive

Elvis is alive

The best-known conspiracy theory surrounding Elvis is that he didn't die on 16 August 1977. He is allegedly still alive and has been spotted numerous times. The earliest reported sighting was the day after he died, when a man resembling Elvis using the name "Jon Burrows" (an alias Elvis himself had sometimes used) checked in to a flight at Memphis International Airport. At Elvis's funeral, several guests reported discrepancies between Elvis's appearance in life and the body in the coffin: the nose and eyebrows were shaped differently, and the hands were soft rather than calloused, which Elvis's were because of his martial arts practice. Some claimed the body was a wax replica. Even curiouser: the day after his death, a former lover received a rose with a card signed El Lancelot, her pet name for Elvis which she claimed no one else knew.

Why would he do it?

Whatever his reasons may have been, Elvis definitely knew how to fake his own death, because he had, in fact, already done it once before. (He arranged for someone to "shoot" him with a gun that contained blanks and used a mechanism for releasing fake blood.) One motive that has been suggested is that not long before he "died", he had lost around $10 million in a property deal in which the Mafia were involved. The theory goes that in return for testifying against the organized crime ring, the government offered him a new identity and safe relocation. Another idea that has been put forward is that Elvis had become extremely self-conscious about his burgeoning weight and his increasingly poor performances, and "dying" seemed the easiest way out of his faltering show-business career. If Elvis really did fake his own death, we're unlikely to ever find out how or why.

Agent Presley

Numerous other conspiracy theories about Elvis Presley persist, including that the King of Rock 'n' Roll was a CIA agent. Proponents of this theory hold that the CIA used his popularity as cover: no one would ever suspect a global celebrity's home as a headquarters for an international spy network. And yet, as a precaution, the conspiracists claim, the CIA also created an extensive system of tunnels beneath Graceland (still said to be in use today), so that the number of government vehicles coming and going would not cause suspicion. After his death, the state ensured that the mansion remained within the Presley family. Rumour has it that, despite the constant waves of tourists to Graceland, the tunnel network is in continuous use.

The circle of death

Another hypothesis suggests that Elvis killed President John F. Kennedy for hogging media attention. If that is indeed true, then, according to the theorists, it would make sense that John Lennon killed Elvis in a similar pique of jealousy. But if Lennon did do it, then the former Beatle neglected to consider Elvis's influence, because, as the theory would have it, Lennon was in turn assassinated in 1980 by none other than Michael Jackson, an ardent Elvis supporter. And he would have gotten away with it, too, if he hadn't drawn attention to himself and given the whole thing away by marrying Elvis' daughter, Lisa Marie Presley. Maybe it didn't end there. Maybe Jackson later met his own fate at the hands of a vengeful Lennon fan. Or could it even have been one of the remaining members of The Beatles?

CHEMTRAILS

WHO:

A shadowy US-government-led cartel

WHEN:

1996–present

WHAT:

Aircraft regularly spray harmful
substances over the world's
population for malicious purposes

How it began

In 1996, the United States Air Force (USAF) published a report about weather modification. Soon after, conspiracy theories began to assert that the USAF was "spraying the US population with mysterious substances" from aircraft "generating unusual contrail patterns". Richard Finke and William Thomas posted such theories on internet forums, their ideas among many other conspiracy theories popularized by late-night radio host Art Bell, starting in 1999. As the chemtrail speculations spread, federal officials were flooded with angry calls and letters from members of the public, prompting the publication of an official report to dispel the rumours in 2000. It was compiled by the Environmental Protection Agency (EPA), the Federal Aviation Administration (FAA), the National Aeronautics and Space Administration (NASA) and the National Oceanic and Atmospheric Administration (NOAA). Many of the theorists took this report to be evidence of a government cover-up. The EPA refreshed its posting in 2015.

What is the theory?

Subscribers to the theory believe that aircraft are regularly spraying harmful substances over the world's population. The chemtrails look like the harmless condensation, or contrails, generated by normal commercial planes. Conspiracists believe that the chemtrails technology is a product of the Reagan administration's Star Wars weaponry of the 1980s, and that it is now being used by a shadowy US-government-led cartel to control the global population. With living space and natural resources on Earth dwindling fast, overpopulation is becoming an increasingly serious problem. And so, the theorists claim, these shadowy groups are using chemtrails to spread virulent life-threatening infectious diseases such as the H1N1 and SARS viruses, said to have been developed in secret laboratories.

An environmental concern

Alongside the use of chemtrails for population control, the theorists claim that national parks across the world are being prepared to act as biospheres to perpetuate animal life ready for "the new global dawn", when the human population will have been reduced to just a fraction of its current size. Environmentally-minded theorists are suspicious that right-wing corporations and politicians are using chemtrails to mask the impact of greenhouse gases on global warming. According to the theorists, sulphur is burned in the stratosphere, creating a cool haze which has a positive short-term effect in maintaining the planet's temperature. This allows major industries to continue their polluting practices rather than opting for ecologically-friendly alternatives that might reduce their profit margins. They call this process "global dimming".

A product of HAARP?

Other theorists point the finger at the High-frequency Active Auroral Research Program (HAARP), claiming that chemtrails are part of an electromagnetic weather-conditioning weapon developed by the US government as part of the programme. This theory connects the oil industry with figures within government, asserting that the weapon is used to further these interests. One such example is the Boxing Day tsunami, where chemtrails were part of a plan to trigger the massive wave in the Indian Ocean, allowing the interested parties to gain access to the oil-rich Indonesian province of Aceh. Another example is Hurricane Katrina, thought to have been magnified by the weapon. The ensuing chaos halted a large volume of domestic crude oil and gas production in the surrounding areas, allowing US oil companies to drive up their prices.

WHO:

The US government

WHEN:

September 2001

WHAT:

The US government either had a hand
in planning the 9/11 attacks or failed
to act on intelligence to stop them

How it began

The events of 11 September 2001, when two planes were hijacked and flown into the twin towers of the World Trade Center in New York, shocked the world. It wasn't long before rumours started that the US government was complicit in the terrorist attacks. Why? Because they allegedly wanted to raise public support for the War on Terror that they pursued in the aftermath. Similar claims have been made about the attack on Pearl Harbor, which some believe US officials allowed to take place to further the war aims of President Roosevelt. Theorists have pointed to the "Project for a New American Century", a strategic document put forward by a group of neoconservative politicians and diplomats in September 2000. It outlined a new approach for US global dominance. One section detailed the readjustment of US military forces across the globe, which, the report stated, could only be done incrementally, unless there happened to be "some catastrophic and catalysing event like a new Pearl Harbor".

A government plot?

If the US government were somehow involved, it raises the question of how such an elaborate assault could have been prepared and executed in secret. A widely discussed theory is that the US intelligence agencies were forewarned that Osama bin Laden and al-Qaeda were planning to attack, but did not act upon the information they received to prevent them. The fact that the CIA and New York City counterterrorism offices, based in Building 7 of the World Trade Center, were destroyed, along with any potentially incriminating evidence, certainly muddies the waters. Another detail that conspiracists often mention is that the greatest amount of seismic activity was recorded as occurring immediately *before* the towers collapsed, and not when they hit the ground. Could this mean that the towers were in fact blown up with explosives planted underneath the buildings? The way the towers imploded instead of collapsing sideways has been cited as evidence to support this theory.

A web of questions

As well as the two planes that hit the World Trade Center, another hit the Pentagon building in Washington DC and a fourth plane crashed in a field near Shanksville, Pennsylvania, after the passengers revolted. Theorists have had a lot of questions to ask about these, too, such as:

- Why did the plane hit the one side of the Pentagon that was empty owing to refurbishment?
- Why was there no wreckage of an airliner found among the debris?
- Was United Airlines flight 93 (the fourth plane) in fact shot down by a US fighter jet because the passengers had found out the truth about the plot and the government could not allow there to be any survivors?

Curiouser and curiouser

The events of 9/11 have also given rise to some other, stranger speculations, perhaps most bizarre of which is the Wingdings conspiracy, which points to the involvement of Microsoft. The theory was based on the following discovery: if you typed "q33ny" in Microsoft Word, selected the text and changed it to the font "Wingdings", the letters would be transformed into a plane, two buildings, a skull and crossbones, and a Star of David. Proponents of this theory claim that "q33ny" was a flight number of one of the hijacked planes. It wasn't. The theory persisted, however. Additionally, typing "NYC" and changing to the Wingdings font would produce a skull and crossbones, the Star of David and a thumbs-up icon, which theorists have taken to be a message to kill the Jews of New York.

The no planes theory

There is one theory related to the 9/11 attacks that even most conspiracy theorists believe to be preposterous, with some conspiracy theory websites having banned all talk of the matter. Morgan Reynolds, a former chief economist in the Labor Department under the Bush administration, claims that no planes were used in the attacks. And how did he know this? Because, he has said, it would have been physically impossible for the Flights 11 and 175 Boeing planes to have penetrated the steel frames of the Towers. But what about the footage of the planes crashing into the towers that was broadcast worldwide? That's easy: the result of digital compositing. Conspiracist and former British spy David Shayler claims that missiles surrounded by holograms were made to look like planes. If only such hologram technology had indeed been possible at the time, then perhaps the people onboard those ill-fated flights wouldn't have had to needlessly die.

Conclusion

We have come to the end of our foray into the weird and, at times, wonderful world of conspiracy theories, a journey that has taken us from tall tales of shapeshifting reptilian rulers to harrowing accounts of interrogations by mysterious Men in Black, and from controversy surrounding the Covid-19 pandemic to anxiety about what chemicals commercial planes are really spreading above our heads.

Being little in nature, this book has only covered some of the many conspiracy theories to have circulated, and of those featured it has given but an overview of what in many cases can be a confusing, contradictory rabbit hole of information. If you would like to delve into more detail on any of the theories featured or discover more theories to leave you wondering, refer to the "Further Reading" section, where you will find many avenues to continue your learning.

In this modern age of fake news, it is wise to maintain an enquiring mind, but it is also important to keep a balanced view and a firm grip on reality. Remember: the truth is out there. Good luck on your journey of uncovering it.

Further Reading

BOOKS

David Aaronovitch, *Voodoo Histories: How Conspiracy Theory Has Shaped Modern History* (2010)

Michael Barkun, *A Culture of Conspiracy: Apocalyptic Visions in Contemporary America* (2003)

Norman Cohn, *A Warrant for Genocide: The Myth of Jewish-World Conspiracy and the Protocols of the Elders of Zion* (1966)

Philip J. Corso and William J. Birnes, *The Day After Roswell* (1997)

Jodi Dean, *Aliens in America: Conspiracy Cultures from Outerspace to Cyberspace* (1998)

Matthew R. X. Dentith, *The Philosophy of Conspiracy Theories* (2014)

James W. Douglass, *JFK and the Unspeakable: Why He Died and Why It Matters* (2010)

Marcus Gilroy-Ware, *After the Fact?: The Truth About Fake News* (2020)

Jamie King, *Conspiracy Theories: A Compendium of History's Greatest Mysteries and More Recent Cover-Ups* (2020)

Susan Lepselter, *The Resonance of Unseen Things: Poetics, Power, Captivity, and UFOs in the American Uncanny* (2016)

Anna Merlan, *Republic of Lies: American Conspiracy Theorists and Their Surprising Rise to Power* (2019)

Will Sommer, *Trust the Plan: The Rise of QAnon and the Conspiracy That Unhinged America* (2023)

PODCASTS

Conspiracy Theories, hosted by Carter Ror and Molly Jean Brandenburg, Spotify

New Conspiracist, hosted by Jolyon Rubinstein and James Ball

TV DOCUMENTARIES

America's Book of Secrets

Behind the Curve

Bob Lazar: Area 51 and Flying Saucers

JFK: The Smoking Gun

Operation Avalanche

The Plot Against the President

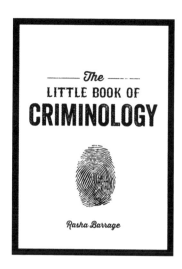

**THE LITTLE
BOOK OF
CRIMINOLOGY**

Rasha Barrage

Paperback

978-1-83799-302-4

Have you always wanted to know what makes an ordinary person commit a crime? Explore the dark side of human nature with this beginner's guide to criminology. From understanding criminal motivation to how crime is policed and prevented, there has never been a more important moment to grasp how crime affects our lives today and how it might tomorrow.

THE LITTLE BOOK OF CULTS

Jamie King

Paperback

978-1-83799-358-1

The strange and disturbing world of cults is fascinating and horrifying in equal measure. Uncover shocking facts about some of the most notorious cults to ever exist, delve into the lives of famous cult leaders and discover the actions and beliefs of cult followers from around the world in this mind-bending book.

Have you enjoyed this book?
If so, find us on Facebook at
SUMMERSDALE PUBLISHERS, on Twitter/X at
@SUMMERSDALE and on Instagram and TikTok at
@SUMMERSDALEBOOKS and get in touch.
We'd love to hear from you!

WWW.SUMMERSDALE.COM

IMAGE CREDITS

Alien © HADI_TRESNANTAN/Shutterstock.com